NATIONAL GEOGRAPHIC

T0040061

Where Do You Live?

Harley Chan

My name is Sasha.
I live in the **United States of America**.
The United States of America looks
like this on a map.

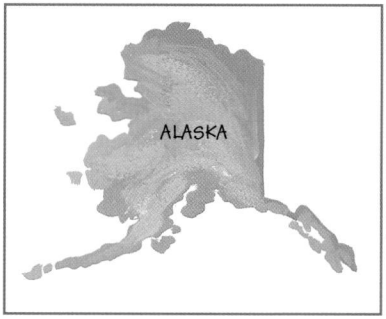

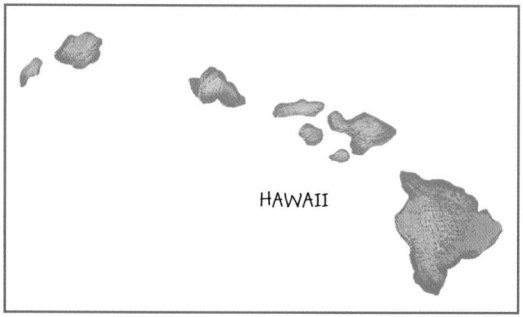

SHINGTON
MONTANA
NORTH DAKOTA
MINNESOTA
NEW HAMPSHIRE
MAINE
VERMONT
MASSACHUSETTS
GON
IDAHO
SOUTH DAKOTA
WISCONSIN
MICHIGAN
NEW YORK
RHODE ISLAND
CONNECTICUT
WYOMING
PENNSYLVANIA
NEW JERSEY
IOWA
NEBRASKA
OHIO
MARYLAND
DELAWARE
EVADA
UTAH
ILLINOIS
INDIANA
WEST VIRGINIA
VIRGINIA
COLORADO
KANSAS
MISSOURI
KENTUCKY
NORTH CAROLINA
TENNESSEE
SOUTH CAROLINA
OKLAHOMA
ARKANSAS
ARIZONA
NEW MEXICO
GEORGIA
MISSISSIPPI
ALABAMA
TEXAS
FLORIDA
LOUISIANA

I live in the state of **Colorado**.

The state of Colorado looks like this on a map.

I live in the city of **Denver**.

The city of Denver looks like this on a map.

I live in Denver, Colorado, in the United States of America.

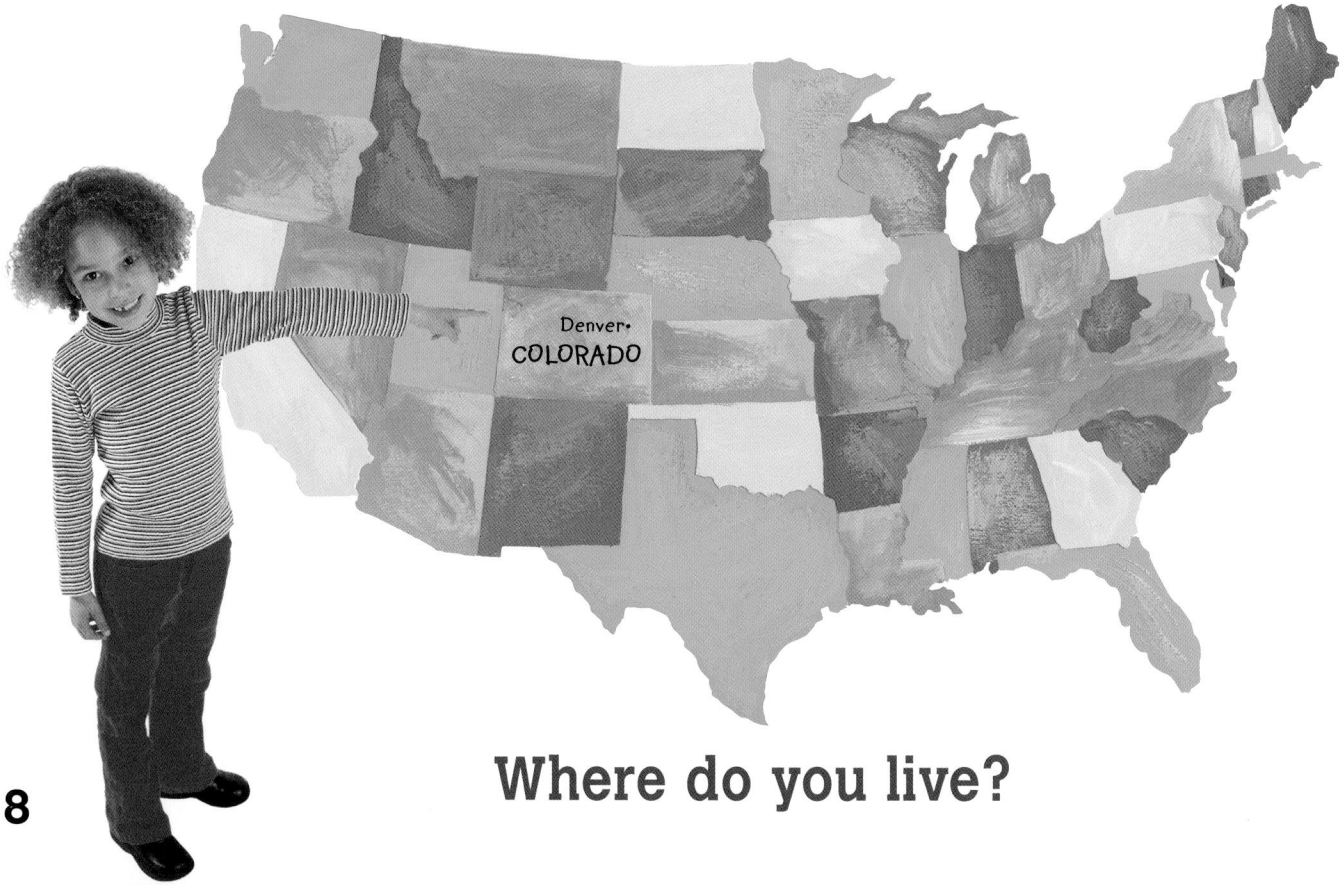

Where do you live?